General Instruction

Materials

Unless instructed otherwise, all projects in this book are stitched on clear 7-count plastic canvas, using Uniek Needloft plastic canvas yarn; Kreinik braids in a variety of weights, including some metallic and glow-in-the-dark styles; and DMC pearl cotton in a variety of weights.

In addition, some designs may call for materials and supplies including:

- ❏ 6-strand cotton embroidery floss
- ❏ Curly wool hair
- ❏ White covered wire
- ❏ Ribbon
- ❏ Wire nippers
- ❏ Thick clear-drying craft glue

Stitches

In addition to the stitches illustrated on page 28, some designs include the Smyrna Cross Stitch, the Smyrna Cross Variation, the Lark's Head Knot, and the Algerian Eye Stitch. Refer to these stitch diagrams for working these stitches.

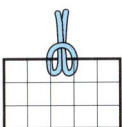

Lark's Head Knot

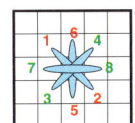

Smyrna Cross

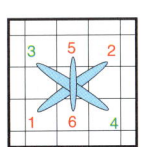

Smyrna Cross Variation

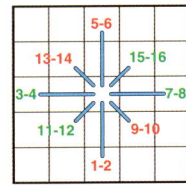

Algerian Eye Stitch

Using Stitched Motifs

You'll find lots of uses for your stitched designs!

- • Cement a Crafter's Choice Mighty Button magnet on the back to make a fridgie magnet.

- • Stitch or glue one to the end of a length of grosgrain ribbon for a bookmark.

- • Use them as tags to help identify luggage, gym bags, etc.

- • Tie or glue them to baskets, small flowerpots, gift packages or other gift containers.

- • Glue one to the blunt end of a long skewer for a plant poke to brighten a bouquet or potted plant.

- • Glue them to the front of handmade greeting cards or gift cards.

Let your imagination run wild!

Celebrating Clock

Size: 4⅛ inches W x 4⅞ inches H (10.5cm x 12.4cm)
Skill Level: Beginner

Materials

- ❏ ¼ sheet clear 7-count plastic canvas
- ❏ Plastic canvas yarn as listed in color key
- ❏ Heavy (#32) braid as listed in color key
- ❏ #5 pearl cotton as listed in color key
- ❏ #16 tapestry needle

Stitching Step by Step

1 Cut one clock from plastic canvas according to graph.

2 Stitch clock according to graph, referring to stitch diagram (above) to work black Smyrna Cross Stitches for musical notes.

3 Overcast edges according to graph.

4 Using black yarn, work two side-by-side Straight Stitches for each eye. Using Christmas red, Straight Stitch nose; using white, Straight Stitch hat highlight with white.

5 Using 1 ply separated from a length of white yarn, Backstitch highlights on hat according to graph, and work tiny highlights in eyes, passing over the right-hand black stitch in each eye.

6 Using gold heavy (#32) braid, Backstitch and Straight Stitch horizontal lines of musical scale, then outlines of musical notes. Backstitch and Straight Stitch accents on clock according to graph.

7 Using black #5 pearl cotton throughout, Backstitch and Straight Stitch remaining details, stitching alongside gold stitches of musical notes, clock hands and face outline. Work French Knots on clock face, wrapping pearl cotton around needle twice.

COLOR KEY		
Yards	**Plastic Canvas Yarn**	
3 (2.7m)	■	Black #00
1 (0.9m)	■	Red #01
2 (1.8m)	■	Christmas red #02
1 (0.9m)	■	Fern #23
2 (1.8m)	■	Eggshell #39
4 (3.6m)	■	White #41
1 (0.9m)	■	Yellow #57
	✳	Black #00 Smyrna Cross Stitch
	╱	Black #00 Straight Stitch
	╱	Christmas red #02 Straight Stitch
	⊠	Fern #23 Cross Stitch
	╱	White #41 full-strand Straight Stitch
	╱	White #41 1-ply Backstitch and Straight Stitch
3 (2.7m)	**Heavy (#32) Braid**	
	⊠	Gold #002 Cross Stitch
	╱	Gold #002 Backstitch and Straight Stitch
3 (2.7m)	**#5 Pearl Cotton**	
	╱	Black #310 Backstitch and Straight Stitch
	●	Black #310 French Knot (2 wraps)

Color numbers given are for Uniek Needloft plastic canvas yarn, Kreinik Heavy (#32) Braid, and DMC #5 pearl cotton.

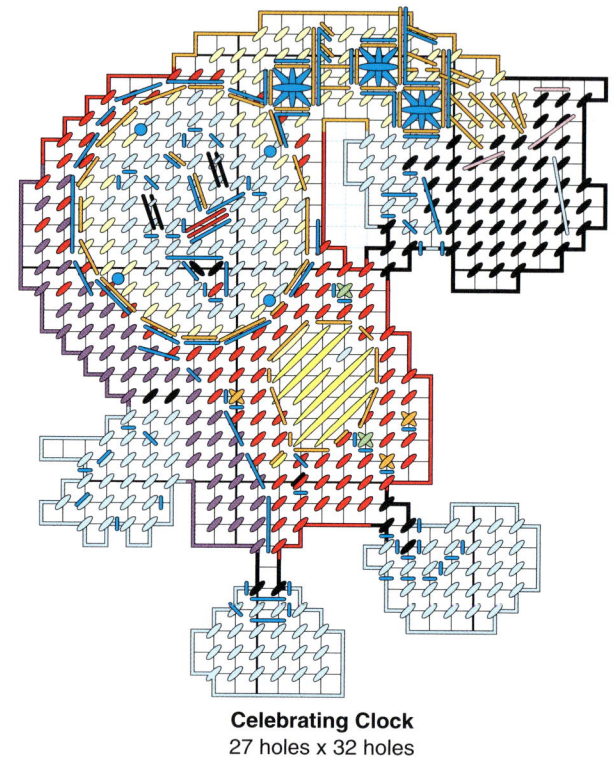

Celebrating Clock
27 holes x 32 holes
Cut 1

Lovey Dovey

Size: 3 inches W x 5½ inches H (7.6cm x 14cm)
Skill Level: Beginner

Materials

- ❑ ¼ sheet clear 7-count plastic canvas
- ❑ Plastic canvas yarn as listed in color key
- ❑ Heavy (#32) braid as listed in color key
- ❑ #5 pearl cotton as listed in color key
- ❑ 2 (14-inch/35.6cm) pieces 30-gauge white-covered stem wire
- ❑ Bamboo skewer
- ❑ #16 tapestry needle
- ❑ Small comb
- ❑ Wire nippers
- ❑ Thick clear-drying craft glue

Stitching Step by Step

1 Cut one bird motif and one of each heart from plastic canvas according to graphs.

2 Stitch bird according to graph, filling in uncoded areas with white Continental Stitches and Overcasting edges according to graph.

3 Using two strands of red hi lustre heavy (#32) braid throughout, stitch hearts and Overcast edges.

4 Using one strand of red hi lustre heavy (#32) braid and referring to Eye Detail graph throughout, Backstitch bird's eyes. Using white yarn, Straight Stitch eyelids. Using black #5 pearl cotton through step 5, Backstitch next to eye stitches.

5 Backstitch and Straight Stitch remaining details according to graph.

6 Using 1 ply separated from a strand of fern yarn, Backstitch and Straight Stitch stems and leaves of bouquet. Using 1 strand of red hi lustre heavy (#32) braid, Straight Stitch highlights in flowers according to graph.

7 *Feather tuft on head:* Referring to stitch diagram (page 1), use 2 strands of white yarn to work Lark's Head Knot at placement point indicated by light blue dot on graph. Trim yarn tails to measure ½ inch (1.3cm). Separate the yarn ends using the tip of the tapestry needle; use comb to fluff.

8 *"Floating" hearts:* Referring to photo throughout, twist lengths of stem wire together to form one 14-inch (35.6cm) length. Bend wire around bamboo skewer to curl. Cut wire into three lengths: long, medium and short. Straighten ½ inch (1.3cm) at both ends of each piece. At one end of each piece, pull straight ends apart to form a "Y." Glue "Y's" arms to the backs of stitched heart; let glue set.

9 Gather opposite ends of wires, forming a bouquet. Using 1 ply separated from a strand of white yarn, Whipstitch wire stems to back of bird motif. Apply a drop of glue over ends of wire stems as you Whipstitch them.

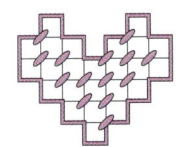

Lovey Dovey Heart
7 holes x 6 holes
Cut 1

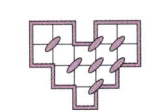

Lovey Dovey Heart
5 holes x 4 holes
Cut 1

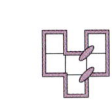

Lovey Dovey Heart
3 holes x 3 holes
Cut 1

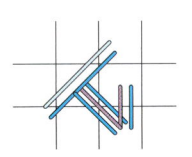

**Lovey Dovey
Eye Detail**

COLOR KEY		
Yards		**Plastic Canvas Yarn**
1 (0.9m)	🟩	Fern #23
3 (2.7m)	🟨	Yellow #57
1 (0.9m)	🟥	Bright orange #58
1 (0.9m)	🟪	Bright pink #62
4 (3.6m)		Uncoded areas are white #41 Continental Stitches
	╱	Fern #23 1-ply Backstitch and Straight Stitch
	╱	White #41 Straight Stitch and Overcast
	○	White #41 2-strand Lark's Head Knot
4 (3.6m)		**Heavy (#32) Braid**
	🟪	Red hi lustre #003HL (2 strands)
	╱	Red hi lustre #003HL 1-strand Backstitch and Straight Stitch
3 (2.7m)		**#5 Pearl Cotton**
	╱	Black #310 Backstitch and Straight Stitch

Color numbers given are for Uniek Needloft plastic canvas yarn, Kreinik Heavy (#32) Braid, and DMC #5 pearl cotton.

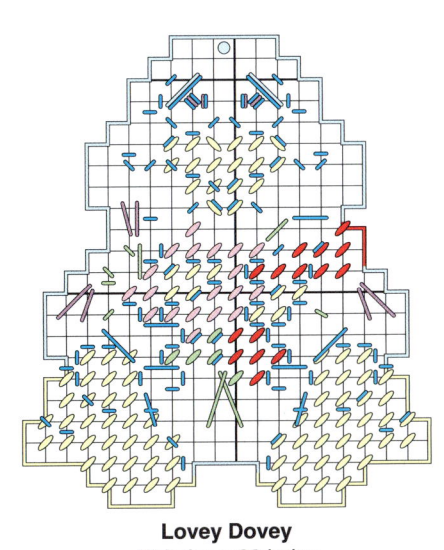

Lovey Dovey
19 holes x 22 holes
Cut 1

Luck o' the Irish

Size: 4¼ inches W x 4½ inches H (10.8cm x 11.4cm)
Skill Level: Beginner

Materials

❏ ¼ sheet clear 7-count plastic canvas
❏ Plastic canvas yarn as listed in color key
❏ #5 pearl cotton as listed in color key
❏ Powdered cosmetic blush
❏ Cotton-tipped swab
❏ #16 tapestry needle

Stitching Step by Step

1 Cut one shamrock from plastic canvas according to graph.

2 Stitch shamrock according to graph, filling in uncoded areas with light peach Continental Stitches. *Note: Leave opening where nose will be stitched directly onto plastic canvas.* Straight Stitch shamrock leaves, stitching twice through each pair of holes and alternating colors as indicated.

3 Overcast edges according to graph.

4 Using black yarn, work two Straight Stitches side by side for open eye. Using white yarn, Backstitch a tiny highlight stitch in eye, between the black stitches. Using rust yarn, Straight Stitch eyebrows.

5 Using fern yarn, Straight Stitch shamrock stem. Using black #5 pearl cotton, Backstitch and Straight Stitch remaining details according to graph.

6 Using a cotton-tipped swab, apply a small amount of powdered cosmetic blush to cheeks.

COLOR KEY	
Yards	**Plastic Canvas Yarn**
1 (0.9m)	■ Black #00
2 (1.8m)	▨ Rust #09
3 (2.7m)	▨ Fern #23
3 (2.7m)	▨ Holly #27
4 (3.6m)	▨ Christmas green #28
2 (1.8m)	Uncoded areas are light peach #56 Continental Stitches
	╱ Black #00 Straight Stitch
	╱ Rust #09 Straight Stitch
	╱ Fern #23 Straight Stitch
	╱ Christmas green #28 Straight Stitch
	╱ Light peach #56 Straight Stitch
1 (0.9m)	╱ White #41 Backstitch
	#5 Pearl Cotton
2 (1.8m)	╱ Black #310 Backstitch and Straight Stitch
Color numbers given are for Uniek Needloft plastic canvas yarn and DMC #5 pearl cotton.	

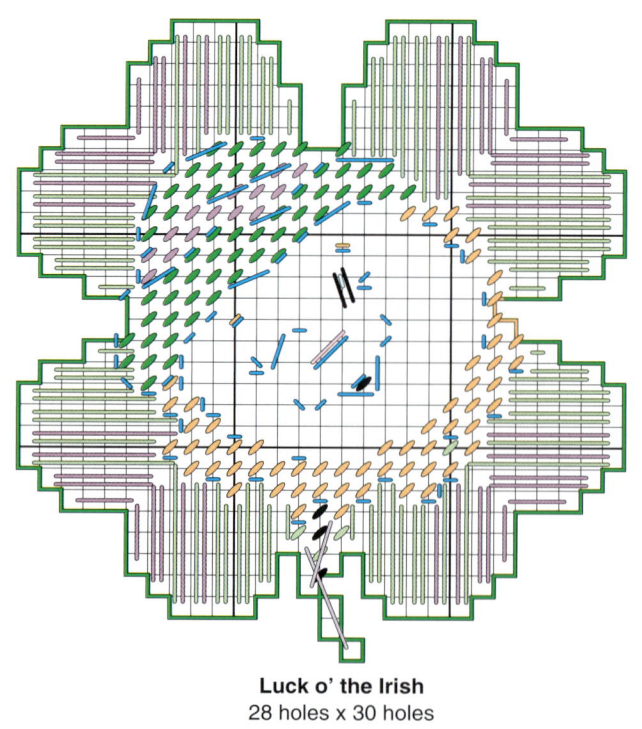

Luck o' the Irish
28 holes x 30 holes
Cut 1

Egg Cottage

Size: 3¼ inches W x 5 inches H (8.2cm x 12.7cm)
Skill Level: Beginner

Materials
❑ ¼ sheet clear 7-count plastic canvas
❑ Plastic canvas yarn as listed in color key
❑ #3 pearl cotton as listed in color key
❑ #5 pearl cotton as listed in color key
❑ Tapestry needles: #16 and #18

Stitching Step by Step

1 Cut one egg cottage from plastic canvas according to graph.

2 Using #16 tapestry needle through step 6, stitch egg cottage according to graph, filling in uncoded areas with pink Continental Stitches.

3 Overcast edges according to graph.

4 Using yellow yarn, work doorknob with large crossing Straight Stitches. Using white yarn, Straight Stitch ears and finial. Using pink yarn, work two small side-by-side stitches for nose.

5 Using 1 ply separated from a length of black yarn, work French Knot eyes, wrapping yarn around needle once.

6 Using white #3 pearl cotton throughout, Backstitch and Straight Stitch details as indicated on graph, passing under the vertical yarn stitch on finial. Form French Knots according to graph, wrapping pearl cotton around needle twice.

7 Using #18 tapestry needle and white #3 pearl cotton, work a tiny highlight stitch in each eye, drawing the pearl cotton up behind the French Knot, around the top edge of the knot, and piercing the knot as you draw it back down through the center.

8 Using dark beaver gray #5 pearl cotton, Backstitch and Straight Stitch remaining details according to graph.

9 Using #16 tapestry needle and lavender and pink yarns according to graph, work French Knots in centers of flowers, wrapping yarn around needle once.

COLOR KEY		
Yards	**Plastic Canvas Yarn**	
1 (0.9m)	■ Black #00	
1 (0.9m)	Lavender #05	
1 (0.9m)	Tangerine #11	
2 (1.8m)	Moss #25	
1 (0.9m)	Baby blue #36	
3 (2.7m)	White #41	
1 (0.9m)	Lilac #45	
2 (1.8m)	Yellow #57	
2 (1.8m)	Uncoded areas are pink #07 Continental Stitches	
	╱ Pink #07 Backstitch	
	╱ White #41 Straight Stitch	
	╱ Yellow #57 Straight Stitch	
	● Black #00 1-ply French Knot (1 wrap)	
	● Lavender #05 French Knot (1 wrap)	
	○ Pink #07 French Knot (1 wrap)	
#3 Pearl Cotton		
1 (0.9m)	╱ White Backstitch and Straight Stitch	
	● White French Knot (2 wraps)	
#5 Pearl Cotton		
3 (2.7m)	╱ Dark beaver gray #646 Backstitch and Straight Stitch	

Color numbers given are for Uniek Needloft plastic canvas yarn, and DMC #3 and #5 pearl cotton.

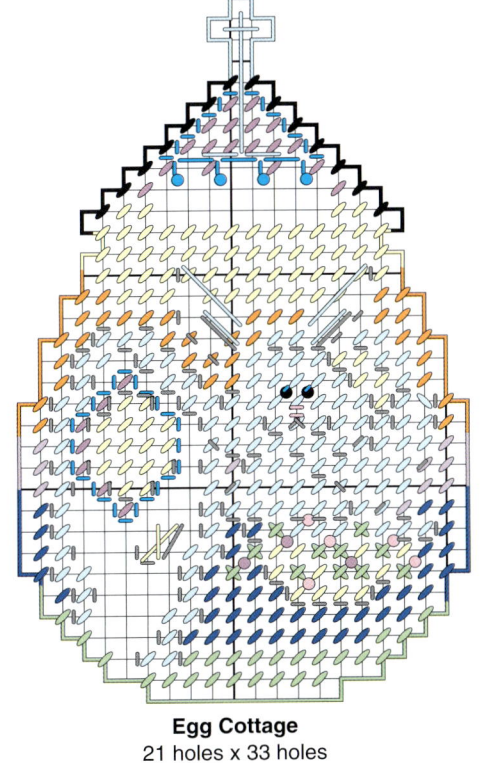

Egg Cottage
21 holes x 33 holes
Cut 1

Cross & Lamb

Size: 3¾ inches W x 4⅞ inches H (9.5cm x 12.4cm)
Skill Level: Beginner

Materials

- ❑ ¼ sheet almond 7-count plastic canvas
- ❑ Plastic canvas yarn as listed in color key
- ❑ Medium (#16) braid as listed in color key
- ❑ Heavy (#32) braid as listed in color key
- ❑ #3 pearl cotton as listed in color key
- ❑ #5 pearl cotton as listed in color key
- ❑ Tapestry needles: #16 and #18

Stitching Step by Step

1 Cut one cross-and-lamb motif from plastic canvas according to graph.

2 Using #16 tapestry needle through step 5, stitch cross and lamb. Overcast edges according to graph, noting that uncoded edges of cross are not Overcast.

3 Using antique gold medium (#16) braid, Backstitch edges of cross. Using gold heavy (#32) braid throughout, refer to stitch diagram (page 1) to stitch Algerian Eye Stitch in center of cross. Work fan-shaped groups of Straight Stitches on ends of cross, beginning with the outermost stitches on each set and working toward the center.

4 Using black #5 pearl cotton throughout, Backstitch lamb's ears and face, passing over the nose four times. Work French Knot eyes wrapping the pearl cotton around the needle twice.

5 Using dark beaver gray #5 pearl cotton throughout, Backstitch and Straight Stitch features according to graph.

6 Using #18 tapestry needle and white #3 pearl cotton throughout, work a tiny highlight stitch in each eye, drawing the pearl cotton up behind the French Knot, around the top edge of the knot, and piercing the knot as you draw it back down through the center.

7 Work Straight Stitches according to graph. Work French Knots on lamb and flowers, wrapping pearl cotton around needle once.

COLOR KEY

Yards	Plastic Canvas Yarn
1 (0.9m)	■ Black #00
1 (0.9m)	■ Pink #07
1 (0.9m)	■ Moss #25
1 (0.9m)	■ Baby blue #36
2 (1.8m)	■ Eggshell #39
2 (1.8m)	■ Beige #40
2 (1.8m)	■ White #41
1 (0.9m)	■ Yellow #57
Medium (#16) Braid	
1 (0.9m)	╱ Antique gold #205C Backstitch
Heavy (#32) Braid	
1 (0.9m)	✳ Gold #002 Algerian Eye Stitch
	╱ Gold #002 Straight Stitch
#3 Pearl Cotton	
2 (1.8m)	╱ White #41 Backstitch and Straight Stitch
	● White #41 French Knot (1 wrap)
#5 Pearl Cotton	
1 (0.9m)	╱ Black #310 Backstitch and Straight Stitch
1 (0.9m)	╱ Dark beaver gray #646 Backstitch and Straight Stitch
	● Black #310 French Knot (2 wraps)

Color numbers given are for Uniek Needloft plastic canvas yarn, Kreinik Medium (#16) Braid and Heavy (#32) Braid, and DMC #3 and #5 pearl cotton.

Cross & Lamb
24 holes x 32 holes
Cut 1

Mother's Day

Size: 3⅜ inches W x 4¼ inches H (8.6cm x 10.8cm)
Skill Level: Beginner

Materials

❏ ¼ sheet clear 7-count plastic canvas
❏ Plastic canvas yarn as listed in color key
❏ #3 pearl cotton as listed in color key
❏ #8 pearl cotton as listed in color key
❏ Tapestry needles: #16 and #18

Stitching Step by Step

1 Cut one Mother's Day kittens motif from plastic canvas according to graph.

2 Using #16 tapestry needle through step 5, stitch plastic canvas according to graph, filling in uncoded areas with silver Continental Stitches.

3 Overcast edges according to graph.

4 Using pink yarn, work two Straight Stitches side by side for each nose. Using white yarn, Straight Stitch decorative flourishes on cupboard. Using 1 ply separated from a length of cinnamon yarn, Straight Stitch spoon handle.

5 Using white #3 pearl cotton, Straight Stitch "MOM" on heart. Using black #8 pearl cotton throughout, Backstitch and Straight Stitch other details indicated by black lines on graph. Using 2 strands of black #8 pearl cotton, work French Knot eyes, wrapping pearl cotton around needle twice.

6 Using white #3 pearl cotton throughout, Backstitch and Straight Stitch noses and apron. Using #18 tapestry needle, work a tiny highlight stitch in each eye, drawing the pearl cotton up behind the French Knot, around the top edge of the knot, and piercing the knot as you draw it back down through the center.

COLOR KEY

Yards	Plastic Canvas Yarn
1 (0.9m)	■ Christmas red #02
2 (1.8m)	■ Pink #07
1 (0.9m)	■ Cinnamon #14
1 (0.9m)	■ Fern #23
1 (0.9m)	■ Gray #38
1 (0.9m)	■ White #41
2 (1.8m)	■ Yellow #57
1 (0.9m)	■ Bright blue #60
3 (2.7m)	Uncoded areas are silver #37 Continental Stitches
	⁄ Silver #37 Overcast
	⁄ Pink #07 Backstitch and Straight Stitch
	⁄ Cinnamon #14 1-ply Straight Stitch
	⁄ White #41 Straight Stitch
#3 Pearl Cotton	
1 (0.9m)	⁄ White Backstitch and Straight Stitch
#8 Pearl Cotton	
4 (3.6m)	⁄ Black #310 Backstitch and Straight Stitch
	● Black #310 2-strand French Knot (2 wraps)

Color numbers given are for Uniek Needloft plastic canvas yarn, and DMC #3 and #8 pearl cotton.

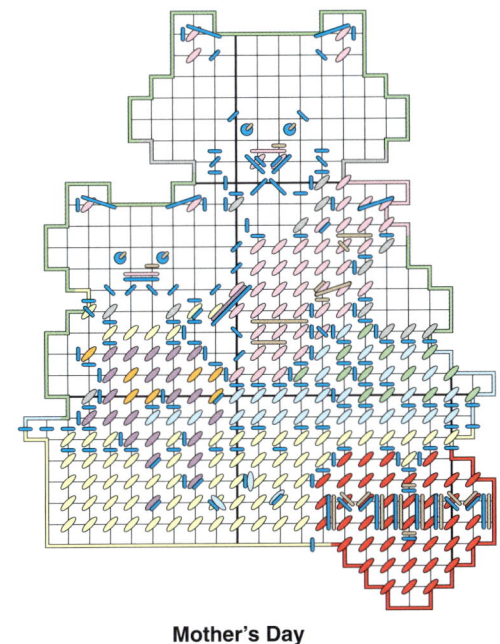

Mother's Day
22 holes x 28 holes
Cut 1

Father's Day

Size: 3⅜ inches W x 4⅛ inches H (8.6cm x 10.5cm)
Skill Level: Beginner

Materials

❏ ¼ sheet clear 7-count plastic canvas
❏ Plastic canvas yarn as listed in color key
❏ #3 pearl cotton as listed in color key
❏ #5 pearl cotton as listed in color key
❏ Tapestry needles: #16 and #18

Stitching Step by Step

1 Cut one Father's Day teddy bears motif from plastic canvas according to graph.

2 Using #16 tapestry needle through step 6, stitch teddy bears according to graph, filling in uncoded areas with beige Continental Stitches.

3 Overcast edges according to graph.

4 Using black yarn, work two side-by-side Straight Stitches for pole handle below little bear's arm.

5 Using black #5 pearl cotton throughout, Backstitch and Straight Stitch other details according to graph. Work French Knot eyes, wrapping pearl cotton around needle three times.

6 Using white #3 pearl cotton through step 7, work Straight Stitches to fill reel, passing over each stitch four times. Backstitch and Straight Stitch top of reel, nose and handle highlights, "Dad" and fishing line.

7 Using #18 tapestry needle, work a tiny highlight stitch in each eye, drawing the pearl cotton up behind the French Knot, around the top edge of the knot, and piercing the knot as you draw it back down through the center.

8 Using Christmas red yarn, Straight Stitch edge of reel and broken pole.

9 Using black #5 pearl cotton, Backstitch and Straight Stitch "shadow" accents of reel, fishing line, pole and letters.

COLOR KEY

Yards	Plastic Canvas Yarn
1 (0.9m)	☐ Black #00
1 (0.9m)	🟥 Christmas red #02
1 (0.9m)	☐ Royal #32
2 (1.8m)	🟫 Camel #43
1 (0.9m)	🟪 Dark royal #48
1 (0.9m)	🟧 Bright orange #58
4 (3.6m)	Uncoded areas are beige #40 Continental Stitches
	╱ Beige #40 Overcast
	╱ Black #00 Straight Stitch
	╱ Christmas red #02 Straight Stitch
	#3 Pearl Cotton
2 (1.8m)	╱ White Backstitch and Straight Stitch
	#5 Pearl Cotton
3 (2.7m)	╱ Black #310 Backstitch and Straight Stitch
	● Black #310 French Knot (3 wraps)

Color numbers given are for Uniek Needloft plastic canvas yarn, and DMC #3 and #5 pearl cotton.

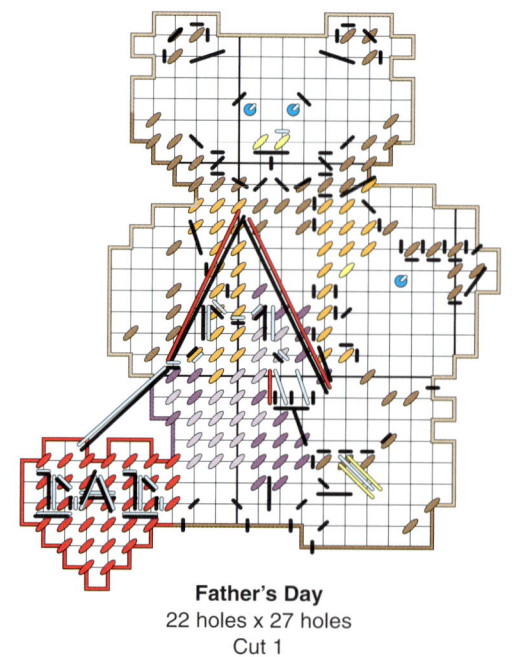

Father's Day
22 holes x 27 holes
Cut 1

Patriot Eagle

Size: 3¼ inches W x 4⅞ inches H (8.2cm x 12.4cm)
Skill Level: Beginner

Materials

❑ ¼ sheet clear 7-count plastic canvas
❑ Plastic canvas yarn as listed in color key
❑ Heavy (#32) braid as listed in color key
❑ #3 pearl cotton as listed in color key
❑ #5 pearl cotton as listed in color key
❑ #16 tapestry needle

Stitching Step by Step

1 Cut one eagle from plastic canvas according to graph.

2 Stitch plastic canvas according to graph, filling in uncoded areas with camel Continental Stitches.

3 Overcast edges according to graph.

4 Using black yarn, work two side-by-side Straight Stitches for each eye. Using white #3 pearl cotton, work a tiny highlight stitch in each eye, between the black stitches.

5 Using dark royal yarn, Backstitch vest shoulder. Using white, Straight Stitch stripes on hat. Using red yarn throughout, work two side-by-side Straight Stitches for center of bow tie. Referring to Hat Brim Detail graph, Straight Stitch hat brim, overlapping stitches as shown.

6 Using black #5 pearl cotton throughout, Backstitch and Straight Stitch remaining details indicated by black lines on graph. Using white #3 pearl cotton, Backstitch and Straight Stitch remaining details, and work French Knots, wrapping pearl cotton around needle once.

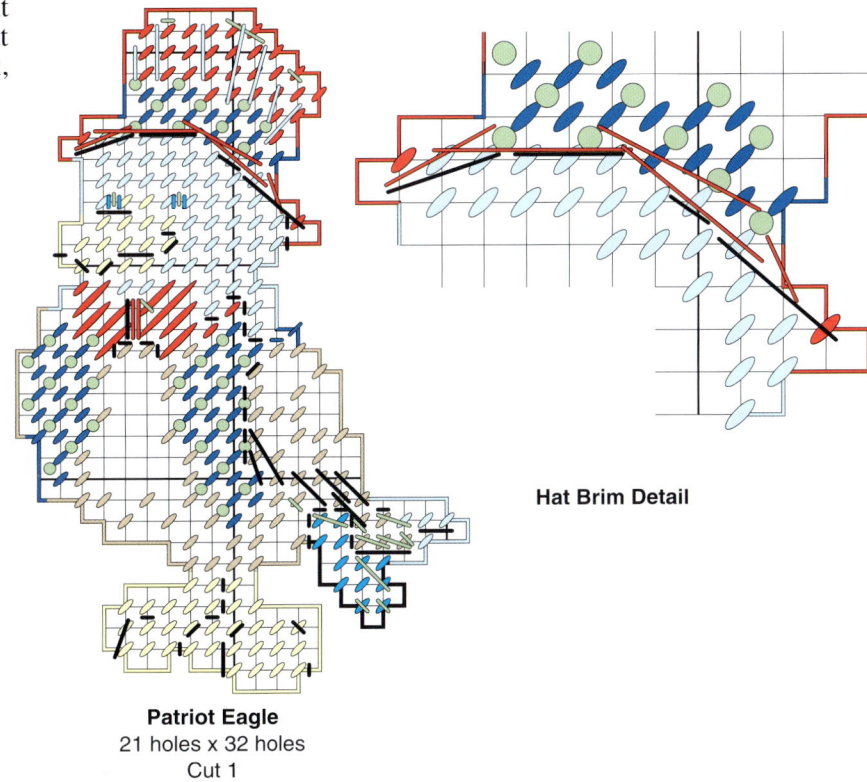

Hat Brim Detail

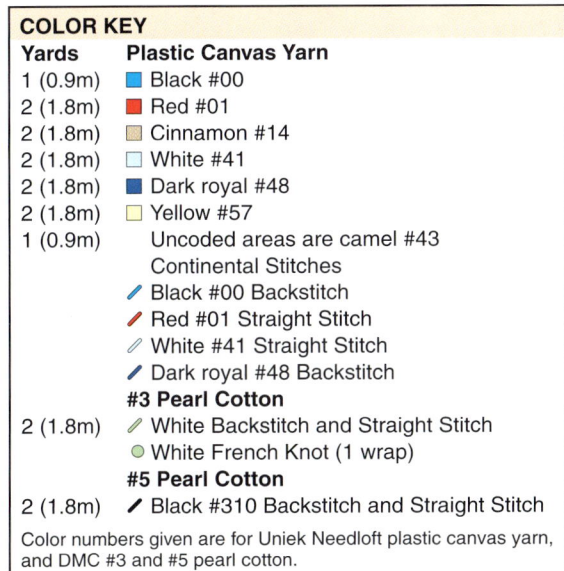

Patriot Eagle
21 holes x 32 holes
Cut 1

COLOR KEY	
Yards	**Plastic Canvas Yarn**
1 (0.9m)	■ Black #00
2 (1.8m)	■ Red #01
2 (1.8m)	■ Cinnamon #14
2 (1.8m)	□ White #41
2 (1.8m)	■ Dark royal #48
2 (1.8m)	□ Yellow #57
1 (0.9m)	Uncoded areas are camel #43 Continental Stitches
	╱ Black #00 Backstitch
	╱ Red #01 Straight Stitch
	╱ White #41 Straight Stitch
	╱ Dark royal #48 Backstitch
	#3 Pearl Cotton
2 (1.8m)	╱ White Backstitch and Straight Stitch
	● White French Knot (1 wrap)
	#5 Pearl Cotton
2 (1.8m)	╱ Black #310 Backstitch and Straight Stitch

Color numbers given are for Uniek Needloft plastic canvas yarn, and DMC #3 and #5 pearl cotton.

Trick-or-Treat Pumpkin

Size: 3⅞ inches W x 4⅞ inches H (9.8cm x 12.4cm)
Skill Level: Beginner

Materials

❏ ¼ sheet clear 7-count plastic canvas
❏ Plastic canvas yarn as listed in color key
❏ Heavy (#32) braid as listed in color key
❏ #3 pearl cotton as listed in color key
❏ #5 pearl cotton as listed in color key
❏ #16 tapestry needle

Stitching Step by Step

1 Cut one jack-o'-lantern motif from plastic canvas according to graph.

2 Stitch plastic canvas according to graph, filling in uncoded areas with bright orange Continental Stitches, and using two strands of tangerine heavy (#32) braid to work Continental Stitches.

3 Overcast edges according to graph.

4 Using 1 ply separated from a strand of black yarn, Straight Stitch right eye and mouth. Using tangerine #3 pearl cotton throughout, Backstitch and Straight Stitch

"Trick or Treat" on bag. Work French Knot, wrapping pearl cotton around needle once.

5 Using black #5 pearl cotton, Backstitch and Straight Stitch details according to graphs, laying stitches alongside tangerine lettering. Using purple yarn, Straight Stitch hat.

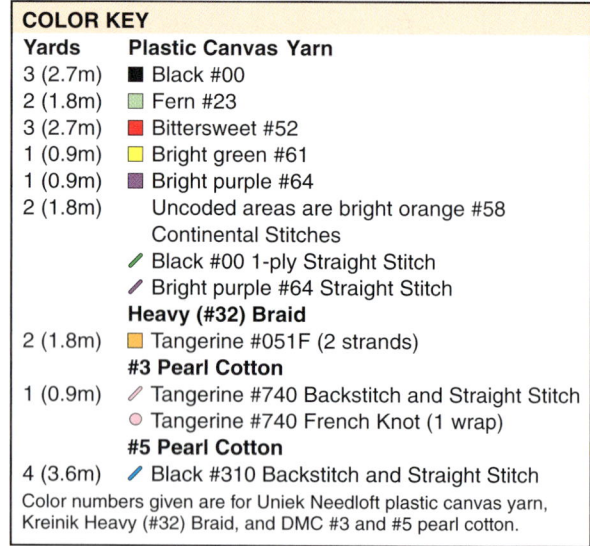

COLOR KEY

Yards	Plastic Canvas Yarn
3 (2.7m)	■ Black #00
2 (1.8m)	▨ Fern #23
3 (2.7m)	▮ Bittersweet #52
1 (0.9m)	▮ Bright green #61
1 (0.9m)	▮ Bright purple #64
2 (1.8m)	Uncoded areas are bright orange #58 Continental Stitches
	╱ Black #00 1-ply Straight Stitch
	╱ Bright purple #64 Straight Stitch
Heavy (#32) Braid	
2 (1.8m)	▮ Tangerine #051F (2 strands)
#3 Pearl Cotton	
1 (0.9m)	╱ Tangerine #740 Backstitch and Straight Stitch
	○ Tangerine #740 French Knot (1 wrap)
#5 Pearl Cotton	
4 (3.6m)	╱ Black #310 Backstitch and Straight Stitch

Color numbers given are for Uniek Needloft plastic canvas yarn, Kreinik Heavy (#32) Braid, and DMC #3 and #5 pearl cotton.

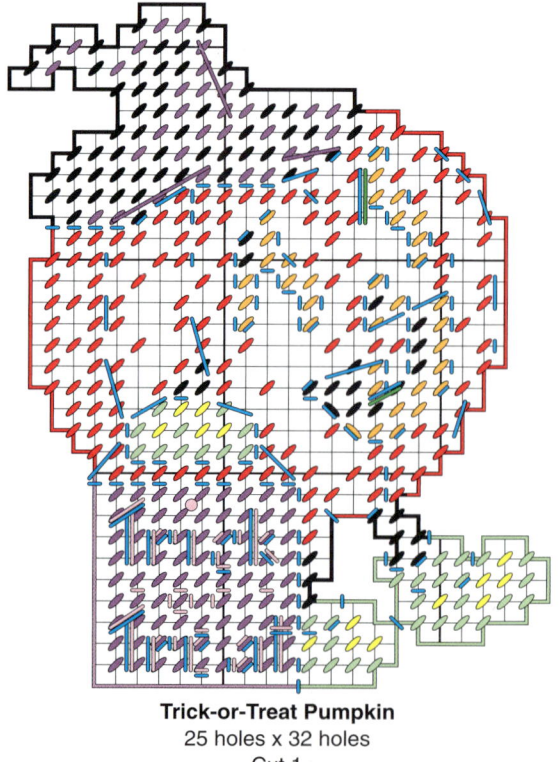

Trick-or-Treat Pumpkin
25 holes x 32 holes
Cut 1

Bertram Bat

Size: 6 inches W x 4⅛ inches H (15.2cm x 10.5cm)
Skill Level: Beginner

Materials

- ¼ sheet clear 7-count plastic canvas
- Plastic canvas yarn as listed in color key
- Heavy (#32) braid as listed in color key
- #3 pearl cotton as listed in color key
- #5 pearl cotton as listed in color key
- Tapestry needles: #16 and #18

Stitching Step by Step

1 Cut one bat from plastic canvas according to graph.

2 Using #16 tapestry needle through step 5, stitch bat according to graph, filling in uncoded areas with Continental Stitches worked with two strands of lemon-lime heavy (#32) braid.

3 Overcast edges according to graph.

4 Using white #3 pearl cotton throughout, Backstitch highlights on bow, shoes and nose. Backstitch fangs, passing over each fang three times.

5 Using black #5 pearl cotton throughout, Backstitch remaining features according to graph. Work French Knots for eyes, wrapping pearl cotton around needle three times.

6 Using #18 tapestry needle and white #3 pearl cotton, work a tiny highlight stitch in each eye, drawing the pearl cotton up behind the French Knot, around the top edge of the knot, and piercing the knot as you draw it back down through the center.

COLOR KEY	
Yards	**Plastic Canvas Yarn**
2 (1.8m)	■ Black #00
1 (0.9m)	□ Fern #23
1 (0.9m)	■ Bright orange #58
2 (1.8m)	■ Bright green #61
1 (0.9m)	■ Bright pink #62
2 (1.8m)	■ Bright purple #64
	Heavy (#32) Braid
3 (2.7m)	Uncoded areas are glow-in-the-dark lemon-lime #054F 2-strand Continental Stitches
	#3 Pearl Cotton
1 (0.9m)	╱ White Backstitch
	#5 Pearl Cotton
4 (3.6m)	╱ Black #310 Backstitch and Straight Stitch
	● Black #310 French Knot (3 wraps)

Color numbers given are for Uniek Needloft plastic canvas yarn, Kreinik Heavy (#32) Braid, and DMC #3 and #5 pearl cotton.

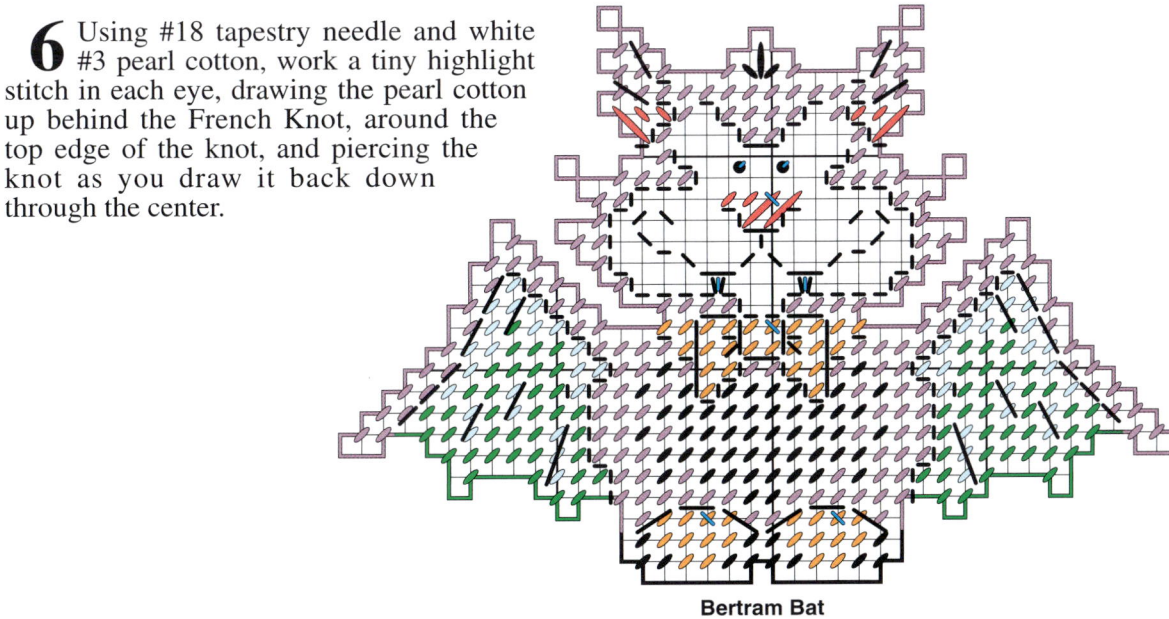

Bertram Bat
39 holes x 27 holes
Cut 1

Turkey

Size: 3⅜ inches W x 4 inches H (8.6cm x 10.2cm)
Skill Level: Beginner

Materials

❑ ¼ sheet clear 7-count plastic canvas
❑ Plastic canvas yarn as listed in color key
❑ #5 pearl cotton as listed in color key
❑ #16 tapestry needle

Stitching Step by Step

1 Cut one turkey from plastic canvas according to graph.

2 Stitch plastic canvas according to graph, filling in uncoded areas with camel Continental Stitches.

3 Overcast edges according to graph.

4 Using black yarn, Straight Stitch eyes.

5 Using 2 strands black #5 pearl cotton, Backstitch and Straight Stitch turkey's smile. Using 1 strand black #5 pearl cotton, Backstitch and Straight Stitch remaining details.

6 Using 1 ply separated from a length of white yarn, Backstitch tiny highlights through eyes, splitting the black Straight Stitch as you draw white yarn down.

```
COLOR KEY
Yards    Plastic Canvas Yarn
1 (0.9m) ■ Black #00
1 (0.9m) ■ Red #01
1 (0.9m) ■ Rust #09
1 (0.9m) ■ Cinnamon #14
2 (1.8m) ■ Beige #40
2 (1.8m) □ White #41
2 (1.8m) ■ Yellow #57
2 (1.8m)   Uncoded areas are camel #43
           Continental Stitches
         ⁄ Black #00 Straight Stitch
         ⁄ White #41 1-ply Backstitch
         ⁄ Camel #43 Overcast
#5 Pearl Cotton
2 (1.8m) ⁄ Black #310 1-strand Backstitch
           and Straight Stitch
         ⁄ Black #310 2-strand Backstitch
           and Straight Stitch
Color numbers given are for Uniek Needloft plastic
canvas yarn and DMC #5 pearl cotton.
```

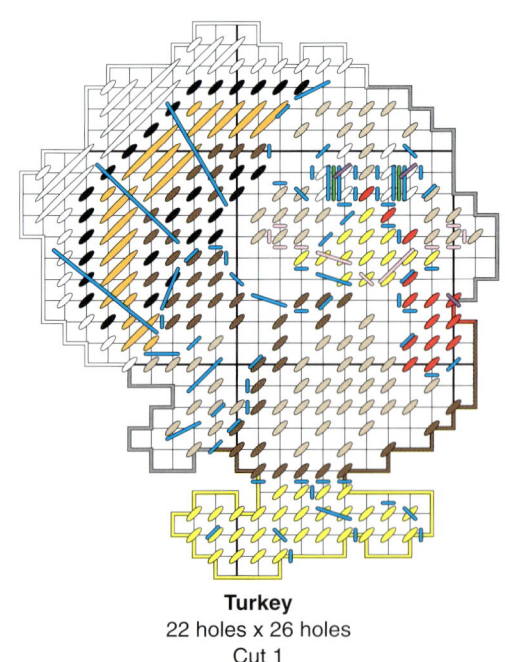

Turkey
22 holes x 26 holes
Cut 1

Candy Snowman

Size: 4½ inches W x 4½ inches H, including fringe
(11.4cm x 11.4cm)

Skill Level: Beginner

Materials

❏ ¼ sheet clear 7-count plastic canvas
❏ Plastic canvas yarn as listed in color key
❏ Medium (#16) braid according to color key
❏ #5 pearl cotton as listed in color key
❏ #16 tapestry needle

Stitching Step by Step

1 Cut one snowman from plastic canvas according to graph.

2 Stitch snowman according to graph, using black yarn to work two stitches side by side for each eye, and using Christmas red yarn to Straight Stitch nose directly onto plastic canvas.

3 Leaving end of scarf unstitched where Lark's Head Knots will be worked, Overcast remaining edges according to graph.

4 Using 1 strand of pearl medium (#16) braid throughout, work Reverse Continental Stitches over

Continental Stitches according to graph. Work a tiny highlight stitch in each eye, between the black stitches. Straight Stitch details on hat.

5 Using dark steel gray #5 pearl cotton, Backstitch and Straight Stitch remaining details according to graph.

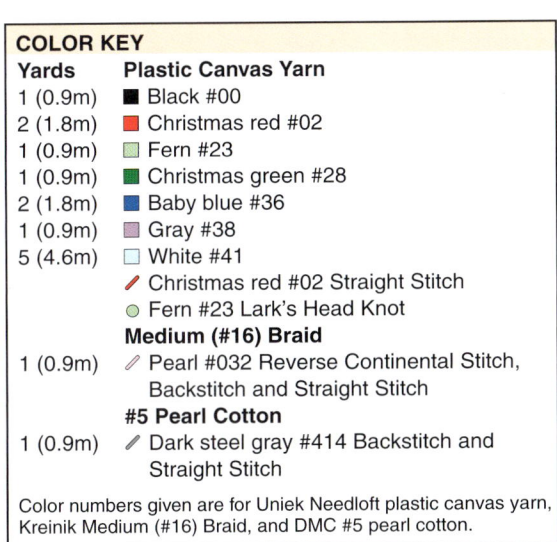

COLOR KEY

Yards	Plastic Canvas Yarn
1 (0.9m)	■ Black #00
2 (1.8m)	■ Christmas red #02
1 (0.9m)	▢ Fern #23
1 (0.9m)	■ Christmas green #28
2 (1.8m)	■ Baby blue #36
1 (0.9m)	▢ Gray #38
5 (4.6m)	▢ White #41
	╱ Christmas red #02 Straight Stitch
	○ Fern #23 Lark's Head Knot
	Medium (#16) Braid
1 (0.9m)	╱ Pearl #032 Reverse Continental Stitch, Backstitch and Straight Stitch
	#5 Pearl Cotton
1 (0.9m)	╱ Dark steel gray #414 Backstitch and Straight Stitch

Color numbers given are for Uniek Needloft plastic canvas yarn, Kreinik Medium (#16) Braid, and DMC #5 pearl cotton.

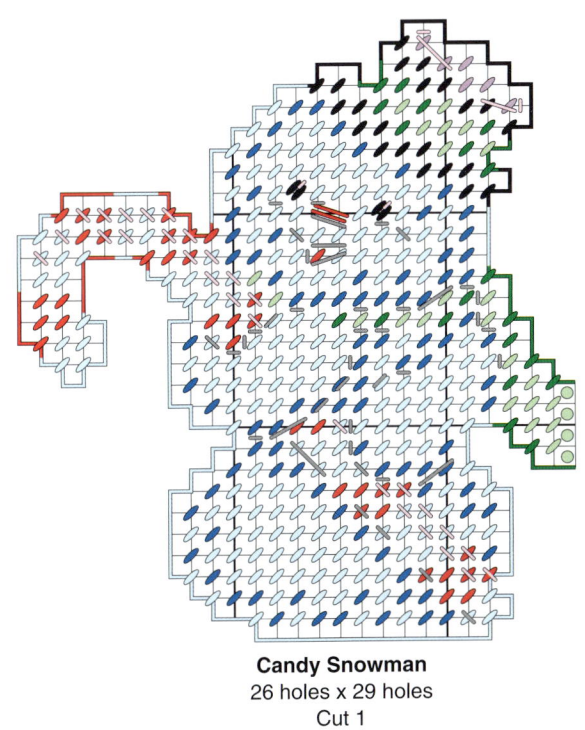

Candy Snowman
26 holes x 29 holes
Cut 1

Woolly Santa

Size: 3⅜ inches W x 4¼ inches H (8.6cm x 10.8cm)
Skill Level: Beginner

Materials

- ¼ sheet clear 7-count plastic canvas
- Plastic canvas yarn as listed in color key
- Heavy (#32) braid as listed in color key
- #5 pearl cotton as listed in color key
- White curly wool hair
- Powdered cosmetic blush
- Cotton-tipped swab
- #16 tapestry needle
- Thick clear-drying craft glue

Stitching Step by Step

1 Cut one Santa from plastic canvas according to graph.

2 Stitch Santa according to graph, filling in uncoded areas with black Continental Stitches.

3 Overcast edges according to graph.

4 Using black yarn, work two Backstitches side by side for each eye. Using 1 ply separated from a strand of white yarn, Backstitch tiny highlights in eyes and on boots. Using a full strand of white yarn, Straight Stitch eyebrows. Using red yarn, work two Straight Stitches for nose.

5 Using gold heavy (#32) braid throughout, work Smyrna Cross Stitch on hat, referring to stitch diagram (page 1). Straight Stitch belt buckle, stitching tongue last so that it lies on top of right-hand stitch on buckle.

6 Using black and medium beaver gray #5 pearl cotton according to graph, work remaining Backstitch and Straight Stitch.

Beard

Note: Do not overwork the curly wool hair. The more it is worked, the less wavy it will be. If overworked, it will look dry and frizzy. When shaping the curly wool hair, you will want the lowest part of the waves for cutting and gluing to the Santa.

1 Cut a 2-inch (5.1cm) piece of curly wool hair. Carefully spread the wool to widen the piece. Separate the top portion to fit the chin from side to side, touching the edges of Santa's hat. Trim center from separated portion to thin the sides, forming a "Y" to fit the face.

2 Spread glue in a smile shape to follow the chin line of the face. Press wool into glue; allow to set.

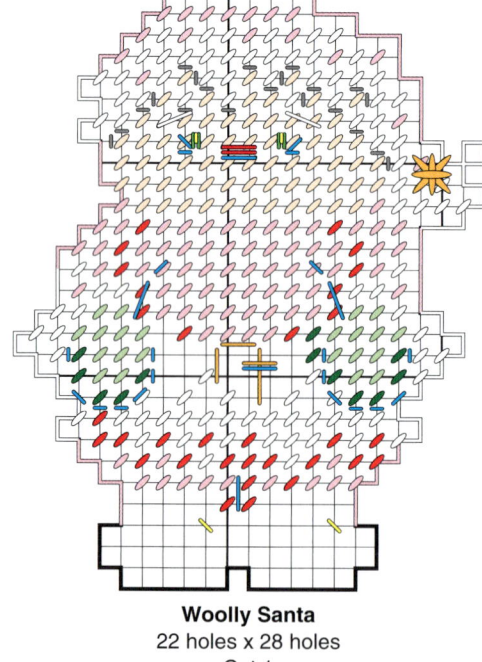

Woolly Santa
22 holes x 28 holes
Cut 1

COLOR KEY	
Yards	**Plastic Canvas Yarn**
1 (0.9m)	■ Red #01
3 (2.7m)	■ Christmas red #02
1 (0.9m)	■ Fern #23
1 (0.9m)	■ Christmas green #28
3 (2.7m)	□ White #41
2 (1.8m)	■ Light peach #56
2 (1.8m)	Uncoded areas are black #00 Continental Stitches
	╱ Black #00 Overcast
	╱ Black #00 Backstitch
	╱ Red #01 Straight Stitch
	╱ White #41 Straight Stitch
	╱ White #41 1-ply Backstitch
Heavy (#32) Braid	
1 (0.9m)	╱ Gold #002 Straight Stitch
	✳ Gold #002 Smyrna Cross Stitch
#5 Pearl Cotton	
1 (0.9m)	╱ Black #310 Backstitch and Straight Stitch
1 (0.9m)	╱ Medium beaver gray #647 Backstitch and Straight Stitch
Color numbers given are for Uniek Needloft plastic canvas yarn, Kreinik Heavy (#32) Braid, and DMC #5 pearl cotton.	

3 Trim lower edge of beard in a rounded shape; glue over tummy.

4 Cut a tiny length of separated wool for mustache. Glue lowest portion of mustache wave below nose; allow to set.

5 Trim mustache ends. Glue cut ends to face to secure.

6 Using a cotton-tipped swab, carefully apply a small amount of powdered cosmetic blush to cheek areas.

Gift Bear

Size: 4¾ inches W x 4½ inches H (12.1cm x 11.4cm)
Skill Level: Beginner

Materials

❑ ¼ sheet clear 7-count plastic canvas
❑ Plastic canvas yarn as listed in color key
❑ #5 pearl cotton as listed in color key
❑ ⅛-inch-wide (0.3cm) red satin ribbon
❑ #16 tapestry needle
❑ Thick clear-drying craft glue

Stitching Step by Step

1 Cut one gift bear motif from plastic canvas according to graph.

2 Stitch bear according to graph, filling in uncoded areas with beige Continental Stitches.

3 Overcast edges according to graph.

4 Using cinnamon yarn, Straight Stitch edges of nose. Using 1 ply separated from a strand of white yarn, Backstitch a tiny highlight on nose, just over top of Straight Stitch.

5 Using ultra dark coffee brown #5 pearl cotton throughout, Backstitch and Straight Stitch remaining details according to graph. Work French Knot eyes, wrapping pearl cotton around needle three times.

6 Tie ribbon in a tiny double bow. Referring to photo, glue bow to bear's neck to left of muzzle.

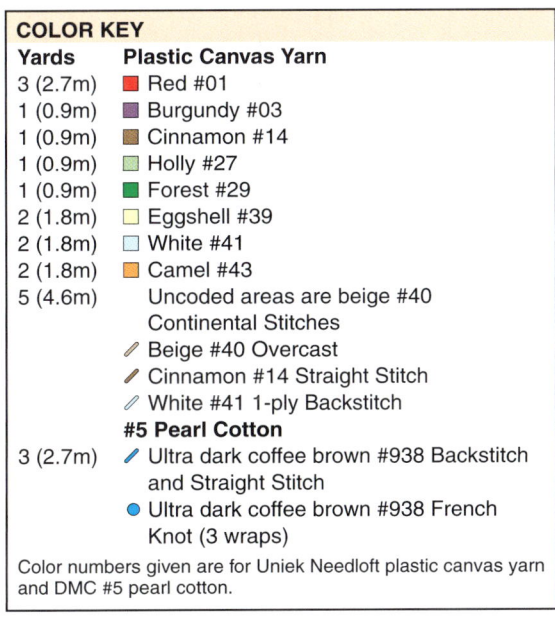

COLOR KEY		
Yards	**Plastic Canvas Yarn**	
3 (2.7m)	■	Red #01
1 (0.9m)	■	Burgundy #03
1 (0.9m)	■	Cinnamon #14
1 (0.9m)	■	Holly #27
1 (0.9m)	■	Forest #29
2 (1.8m)	■	Eggshell #39
2 (1.8m)	■	White #41
2 (1.8m)	■	Camel #43
5 (4.6m)		Uncoded areas are beige #40 Continental Stitches
	∕	Beige #40 Overcast
	∕	Cinnamon #14 Straight Stitch
	∕	White #41 1-ply Backstitch
#5 Pearl Cotton		
3 (2.7m)	∕	Ultra dark coffee brown #938 Backstitch and Straight Stitch
	●	Ultra dark coffee brown #938 French Knot (3 wraps)
Color numbers given are for Uniek Needloft plastic canvas yarn and DMC #5 pearl cotton.		

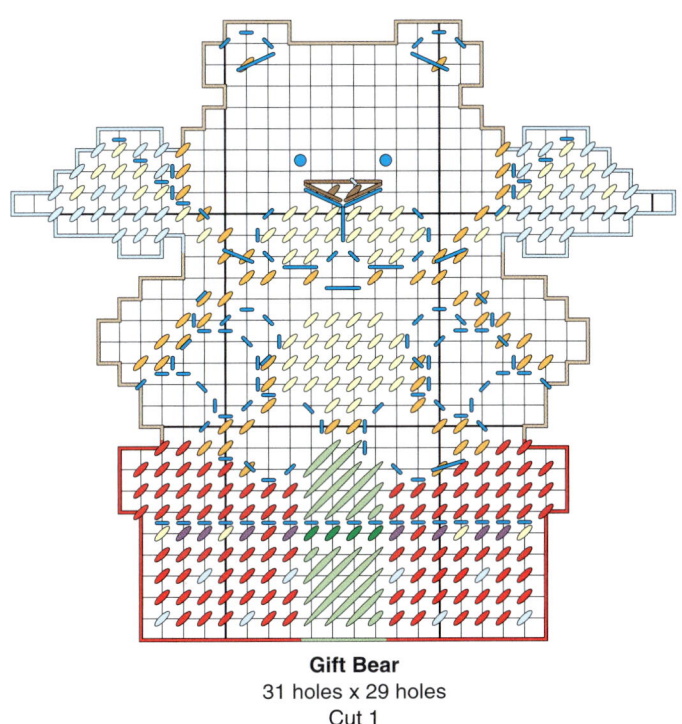

Gift Bear
31 holes x 29 holes
Cut 1

306 E. Parr Road
Berne, IN 46711
www.NeedlecraftShop.com
© 2006 The Needlecraft Shop

The full line of The Needlecraft Shop
products is carried by Annie's Attic catalog.

TOLL-FREE ORDER LINE
or to request a free catalog
(800) 582-6643

Customer Service
(800) 449-0440

Fax (800) 882-6643

Visit www.AnniesAttic.com

ISBN-10: 1-57367-243-2

ISBN-13: 978-1-57367-243-6

Printed in USA

1 2 3 4 5 6 7 8 9

Shopping for Supplies

For supplies, first shop your local craft and needlework stores. Some supplies may be found in fabric, hardware and discount stores. If you are unable to find the supplies you need, please call Annie's Attic at (800) 259-4000 to request a free catalog that sells plastic canvas supplies.

Before You Cut

Buy one brand of canvas for each entire project, as brands can differ slightly in the distance between bars. Count holes carefully from the graph before you cut, using the bolder lines that show each 10 holes. These 10-mesh lines begin in the lower left corner of each graph to make counting easier. Mark canvas before cutting, then remove all marks completely before stitching. If the piece is cut in a rectangular or square shape and is either not worked, or worked with only one color and one type of stitch, we do not include the graph in the pattern. Instead, we give the cutting and stitching instructions in the general instructions or with the individual project instructions.

Covering the Canvas

Bring needle up from back of work, leaving a short length of yarn on back of canvas; work over short length to secure. To end a thread, weave needle and thread through the wrong side of your last few stitches; clip. Follow the numbers on the small graphs beside each stitch illustration; bring your needle up from the back of the work on odd numbers and down through the front of the work on even numbers. Work embroidery stitches last, after the canvas has been completely covered by the needlepoint stitches.

Basic Stitches

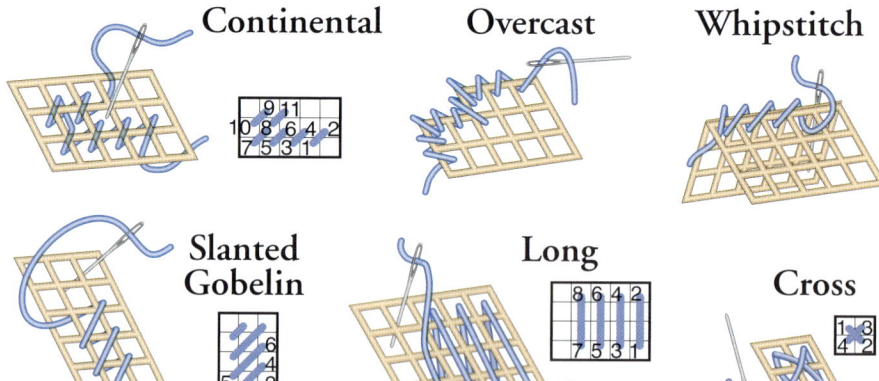

Embroidery Stitches

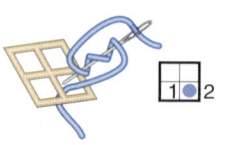

French Knot

Lazy Daisy

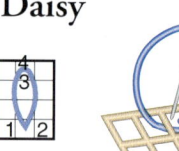

Backstitch

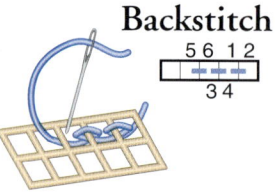

Straight

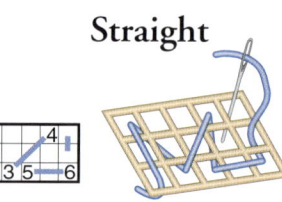

METRIC KEY:
millimeters = (mm)
centimeters = (cm)
meters = (m)
grams = (g)